The Complete Guide to Child Development and Care

C. P. Kumar

Reiki Healer

Roorkee - 247667, India

Disclaimer

While every effort has been made to ensure the accuracy and completeness of the content in this book, the author cannot guarantee that the information contained herein is error-free, up-to-date, or suitable for every individual circumstance.

The author shall not be held liable or responsible for any errors or omissions in the content of the book, nor for any damages, or losses that may arise from any actions taken based upon the suggestions or contents presented in the book.

Readers are advised to use their own judgment and discretion in applying the information provided in this book, and to consult with qualified professionals before taking any action based on the contents of this book. The author disclaims any and all liability or responsibility for any actions taken or not taken based on the information contained in this book.

DEDICATION

To all parents and caregivers, who tirelessly embark on the journey of parenthood, dedicating their love, time, and efforts to shaping the future of our world through the care and development of our children.

Your unwavering commitment to nurturing, protecting, and guiding the little souls in your care is nothing short of extraordinary. Through the sleepless nights and the countless challenges, you stand strong as the pillars of support for your children, helping them flourish in every stage of their growth.

This book, "The Complete Guide to Child Development and Care", is a tribute to your boundless dedication and endless love. Within its pages, we aim to provide you with a comprehensive resource that will aid you in navigating the incredible journey of parenthood.

May this guide serve as a source of knowledge and inspiration, empowering you to create a safe and nurturing environment for your children, right from the newborn stage to their school years and beyond. As you embark on the path of understanding your child's emotional, physical, and intellectual needs, may you find the tools to foster their growth with confidence and compassion.

In every chapter, we acknowledge the profound role you play in shaping the lives of your children. From the tender moments of bonding with your newborn to encouraging creativity and imagination in their play, from promoting healthy habits to supporting their academic journey, your impact is immeasurable.

As you dedicate your heart to your little ones, we also acknowledge the importance of self-care for parents and caregivers. The commitment to your well-being allows you to be the best version of yourself, an even more loving and attentive presence for your children.

To every parent and caregiver, this book is dedicated to your resilience, patience, and unyielding love. May it be a companion, a guide, and a source of reassurance as you embrace the beautiful chaos of parenthood and shape the future generation with love and care.

Lastly, we extend a special dedication to our son Parivesh Kumar, daughter-in-law Preeti Singh, and our 2.5 years old granddaughter Etisha Kumar, who have filled our life with immeasurable joy and love, inspiring me to create this book and share the knowledge of child development and care with all parents and caregivers. May your journey of parenthood be blessed with endless moments of love, growth, and happiness.

With profound gratitude,

C. P. Kumar

CONTENTS

PREFACE

Welcome to "The Complete Guide to Child Development and Care". This book is a comprehensive resource for parents and caregivers, offering valuable insights and practical tips to support children's growth from infancy to early school years.

Parenthood is a remarkable journey filled with joy and challenges. Understanding child development and providing appropriate care can profoundly impact a child's physical, emotional, and cognitive well-being.

From creating a safe environment to fostering emotional intelligence, this guide covers various aspects of child development and parenting. It offers expert advice, real-life experiences, and age-appropriate activities to stimulate growth.

As you embark on this rewarding journey, remember that every child is unique, and the insights shared here can be adapted to suit your child's individual needs.

Thank you for choosing "The Complete Guide to Child Development and Care". We hope it empowers you to provide the best care and support for your child's holistic development. Happy parenting!

C. P. Kumar
Reiki Healer
Former Scientist 'G', National Institute of Hydrology
Roorkee - 247667, India
E-mail: cpkumar@yahoo.com
Web: https://www.angelfire.com/nh/cpkumar/virgo.html

Introduction

Parenthood is a transformative journey, filled with love, challenges, and moments of profound growth. As parents, caregivers, and guardians, we hold a significant responsibility in shaping a child's development and overall well-being. The early years of a child's life are particularly crucial, laying the foundation for their physical, emotional, social, and cognitive development. In this comprehensive guide to child development and care, we will explore the role of parents and caregivers in nurturing children from infancy to adolescence.

The Significance of Early Years

The early years of a child's life, from infancy to early childhood, are often referred to as the formative years. During this period, the child's brain undergoes rapid development, and experiences in the early years have a lasting impact on their future development. Parents and caregivers play a vital role in providing a safe, loving, and stimulating environment that fosters the child's growth.

The Infant Stage

Generally, an infant is a child who is less than 1 year old. This period is characterized by immense dependence on caregivers for all aspects of their care. The bond formed between the infant and their primary caregiver sets the stage for future relationships and emotional development.

Responding to an infant's needs promptly and sensitively promotes a sense of trust and security.

Nurturing the Baby

Babies, typically from birth up to 1 or 2 years old, are in a phase of rapid physical and cognitive development. They explore the world through their senses and learn by imitating adults around them. It is crucial for parents and caregivers to provide a stimulating environment that encourages exploration, promotes motor skills (specific movements of the body's muscles to perform a certain task), and supports language development.

The Toddler's Journey

Toddlers, aged between 1 and 3 years old, are often referred to as "terrible twos" or "threenagers" due to their emerging independence and assertiveness. This phase is marked by significant cognitive and emotional growth, as they learn to communicate, express themselves, and navigate their emotions. Parents and caregivers need to strike a balance between fostering autonomy and providing guidance.

Embracing the Preschool Years

Preschoolers, aged between 3 and 5 years old, are eager learners with boundless curiosity. This is the stage when formal education may begin, and children start to develop social skills through interactions with peers. Parents and caregivers can support their cognitive development by engaging in imaginative play, encouraging creativity, and exposing them to various learning experiences.

Navigating the Middle Childhood

The stage between 6 and 12 years is commonly known as middle childhood. Children in this phase are more independent, forming friendships, and gaining a sense of self-identity. Their academic and extracurricular activities play a crucial role in shaping their interests and skills. Parents and caregivers must provide emotional support, be involved in their education, and foster a sense of responsibility.

Challenges and Strategies

Throughout the journey of parenthood, various challenges arise. From sleepless nights with an infant to dealing with teenage mood swings, each stage presents unique hurdles. Understanding child development, seeking support from a parenting community, and maintaining open communication with the child are essential strategies to overcome these challenges.

The Role of Positive Discipline

Discipline is not synonymous with punishment; rather, it is about teaching children appropriate behavior and values. Positive discipline emphasizes setting clear expectations, offering explanations, and using consequences that promote learning and growth rather than instilling fear. Parents and caregivers should model empathy, respect, and problem-solving skills.

The Impact of Technology

In today's digital age, technology plays a significant role in a child's life. Parents and caregivers must strike a balance between leveraging technology for educational purposes and ensuring that it doesn't hinder their physical activity, social interactions, and overall well-being.

Emotional Support and Mental Health

Mental health is as crucial as physical health in a child's life. Parents and caregivers should be attentive to the child's emotional needs, offer support during challenging times, and seek professional help if necessary. Fostering emotional intelligence can help children navigate their feelings and build resilience.

Creating a Supportive Environment

Family dynamics, community support, and access to resources all contribute to a child's development. Creating a supportive environment where the child feels loved, valued, and safe nurtures their sense of belonging and self-esteem.

Embracing Diverse Perspectives

Children are influenced by their cultural, social, and environmental surroundings. Embracing diversity and promoting inclusive values help children develop empathy, tolerance, and a broader worldview.

Conclusion

Parenthood is an ever-evolving journey that requires continuous learning, adaptability, and love. Understanding the role of parents and caregivers in a child's life is fundamental to raising healthy, happy, and well-adjusted individuals. By providing a nurturing and supportive environment, embracing each child's uniqueness, and being present throughout their developmental stages, we can positively impact their journey of parenthood and set them on a path to a fulfilling and successful life.

Introduction

As parents or caregivers, ensuring a safe and nurturing environment for children is of paramount importance. The home serves as the primary place where children grow, learn, and explore the world around them. Therefore, it is crucial to childproof and design a child-friendly home that encourages their development while safeguarding them from potential hazards. This article aims to provide a comprehensive guide on childproofing and setting up a child-friendly home to promote a safe and enriching environment for children's growth and well-being.

Understanding Child Development and Safety

Before diving into childproofing and setting up a child-friendly home, it is essential to understand child development and how it impacts their interaction with the environment. Children go through various stages of physical, cognitive, and emotional development, which influence their behavior and interests. It is essential to consider the following aspects:

1. Age-appropriate Safety Measures: Tailor your childproofing strategies based on your child's age and developmental milestones. Infants, toddlers, and older children have different safety needs. What works for a toddler may not be suitable for an older child, so understanding their capabilities is crucial.

2. Hazards and Risks: Take the time to identify potential hazards within your home, such as sharp objects, heavy furniture, choking hazards, accessible chemicals, or medications. Understanding these risks allows you to take appropriate measures to mitigate them.

Childproofing Basics

Childproofing involves making necessary modifications to the home environment to minimize risks and prevent accidents. Here are some fundamental childproofing tips:

1. Secure Furniture and Appliances: Anchor heavy furniture, bookshelves, and appliances to the walls to prevent tipping accidents. Children often climb on furniture, and securing them can prevent serious injuries.

2. Install Safety Gates: Use safety gates at stairways and other hazardous areas to restrict access. This prevents young children from wandering into areas where they could get hurt.

3. Childproof Outlets: Cover electrical outlets with safety plugs to prevent electrocution. Children have a natural curiosity, and they may try to stick objects into outlets.

4. Safety Latches and Locks: Apply safety latches and locks on cabinets and drawers containing hazardous items like cleaning supplies, sharp objects, or medications. This prevents accidental ingestion or exposure to dangerous substances.

5. Soften Sharp Corners: Use corner guards to cushion sharp edges of furniture. This minimizes the risk of injuries if a child accidentally runs into furniture.

Creating a Child-Friendly Kitchen

The kitchen is a busy and potentially hazardous area. To make it child-friendly:

1. Lock up Dangerous Items: **Keep sharp knives, cleaning agents, and other harmful objects out of reach in locked cabinets. Childproof locks on cabinets with dangerous items are essential.**

2. Stove Safety: **Use stove knob covers to prevent curious hands from turning on burners. When cooking, use back burners and turn pot handles away from the stove's edge to avoid spills and burns.**

3. Childproof Appliances: **Keep ovens, dishwashers, and refrigerators securely locked when not in use. Children may accidentally turn on appliances or get themselves trapped inside.**

4. Child-Sized Furniture: **Consider adding a child-sized table and chairs in the kitchen, allowing them to participate in meal preparations safely. This fosters a sense of independence and involvement.**

Designing a Safe and Stimulating Playroom

The playroom is an area for exploration and fun. Ensure it's a safe space with these measures:

1. Soft Flooring: **Use padded mats or carpets to minimize injuries from falls. Young children often stumble and fall while playing, and soft flooring provides extra cushioning.**

2. Secure Furniture: **Anchor bookshelves and storage units to the walls to prevent tipping. Children may try to climb on furniture, and securing it keeps them safe.**

3. Age-Appropriate Toys: **Offer toys suitable for your child's age and avoid those with small parts that can pose choking hazards. Regularly inspect toys for signs of wear or damage.**

4. Organized Storage: **Use labeled bins or shelves to encourage tidiness and minimize clutter. Keeping toys organized makes it easier to maintain a safe play environment.**

Childproofing the Bathroom

The bathroom holds several potential dangers, so careful childproofing is crucial:

1. Supervision: **Never leave a young child unattended in the bathroom. Even shallow water can pose a drowning risk.**

2. Secure Toiletries: **Keep medications, toiletries, and cleaning products out of reach in locked cabinets. Many bathroom products are toxic if ingested.**

3. Non-Slip Mats: **Place non-slip mats in the bathtub and on the floor to prevent slips. Bathrooms can become slippery, especially when wet.**

4. Toilet Safety: **Use toilet seat locks to prevent accidental drowning. Children can be top-heavy and easily fall into toilets.**

Bedroom Safety and Comfort

Children spend a significant amount of time in their bedrooms. Here's how to create a safe and cozy sleep environment:

1. Safe Crib: Choose a crib that meets safety standards, and avoid using blankets or pillows until the child is older. Proper sleep environment reduces the risk of Sudden Infant Death Syndrome (SIDS).

2. Window Safety: Install window guards or locks to prevent falls. Children may climb on furniture to reach windows, making window safety crucial.

3. Secure Furniture: Ensure furniture is stable and free from hazards like cords or small objects. Tall furniture like dressers should be anchored to the wall.

4. Night Lights: Use dim night lights to provide comfort and prevent tripping during nighttime visits to the bathroom or parents' room.

Outdoor Safety

Outdoor play is essential for children's development. Ensure a safe outdoor environment with these measures:

1. Secure Play Area: Use soft surfaces like rubber mulch or sand under play equipment to cushion falls. Regularly inspect play structures for loose or damaged parts.

2. Fencing: Install secure fencing around the yard to prevent wandering and keep children away from potential hazards like busy streets.

3. Inspect Play Equipment: **Regularly check and maintain outdoor play equipment for wear and tear. Weather and use can cause deterioration, leading to potential hazards.**

Promoting Exploration and Learning

Beyond childproofing, a child-friendly home should encourage learning and exploration:

1. Reading Corner: **Create a cozy reading nook with age-appropriate books and comfortable seating. Reading fosters imagination and cognitive development.**

2. Art and Craft Area: **Set up a designated space for arts and crafts, equipped with child-safe materials. Artistic expression is essential for creativity and fine motor skill development.**

3. Learning Toys: **Incorporate educational toys and games that stimulate cognitive development. Toys that promote problem-solving and critical thinking can enhance learning.**

4. Sensory Play: **Include sensory play materials like sand, water, or playdough for sensory exploration. Sensory play enhances children's cognitive, emotional, and physical development.**

Conclusion

Creating a safe and nurturing environment is essential for a child's healthy development and well-being. By understanding child development, implementing childproofing strategies, and designing a child-friendly home, parents and caregivers can provide a secure space that promotes exploration, learning, and creativity. A thoughtfully childproofed and child-friendly home will support children in their journey of growth and self-discovery, fostering a sense of security, independence, and happiness.

Introduction

Welcoming a newborn into the world is a beautiful and life-changing experience for parents. However, it also comes with its unique set of challenges. The newborn stage is a critical time when infants undergo rapid physical and emotional development. As parents, understanding how to care for a newborn, establish healthy breastfeeding practices, establish sleep routines, and navigate postpartum challenges is essential for providing the best possible start in life for their little ones. This comprehensive guide will walk you through all aspects of the newborn stage, ensuring that you are well-prepared and confident in your parenting journey.

Caring for a Newborn

During the newborn stage, infants have distinct needs that require special attention. Understanding and meeting these needs are crucial for their overall well-being and development.

1. Feeding Requirements

One of the most critical aspects of caring for a newborn is meeting their feeding requirements. Breastfeeding is highly beneficial for both the baby and the mother. Breast milk provides essential nutrients for the baby's growth and development, as well as antibodies that boost their immune system. For mothers, breastfeeding promotes bonding and releases oxytocin, enhancing the maternal-infant connection. However, if breastfeeding is not possible or desired, bottle-feeding with formula can also provide adequate nutrition for the baby.

2. Diapering and Hygiene

Keeping your newborn clean and comfortable is essential. Regular diaper changes are necessary to prevent diaper rash and discomfort. It's essential to use gentle baby wipes or warm water and cotton balls during diaper changes to avoid skin irritation. Additionally, proper skincare and bathing routines help keep the baby's skin healthy and moisturized.

3. Soothing Techniques

Newborns can often get fussy or restless. Swaddling is a technique that mimics the feeling of being in the womb and can provide comfort to your baby. Understanding your baby's cues for hunger, sleepiness, or discomfort can also help you respond to their needs promptly.

4. Creating a Safe Environment

As your newborn begins to explore the world around them, it's crucial to create a safe environment. Baby-proofing your home involves securing furniture, covering electrical outlets, and keeping hazardous substances out of reach. Additionally, maintaining an appropriate room temperature and dressing your baby in comfortable clothing are essential for their well-being.

Bonding and Communication

Building a strong bond with your newborn fosters trust and security. Effective communication is also vital for understanding your baby's needs.

1. Skin-to-Skin Contact

Skin-to-skin contact, also known as kangaroo care, is a powerful way to bond with your baby. This practice involves placing your baby's naked chest against your bare chest, promoting a sense of security and warmth.

2. Eye Contact and Vocalization

Engaging in eye contact with your newborn and talking or singing to them helps stimulate their cognitive development and communication skills. Babies are naturally drawn to human faces and voices, so these interactions are essential for their social and emotional development.

3. Understanding Crying

Crying is your baby's primary mode of communication. Different cries may indicate hunger, fatigue, discomfort, or other needs. By paying attention to your baby's cues and patterns, you can better understand and respond to their needs.

4. Baby Massage

Infant massage can be a soothing and bonding experience for both parents and babies. Gentle massages can help relax your baby, improve blood circulation, and promote better sleep.

Breastfeeding

Breastfeeding is a natural and essential process that provides numerous benefits for both the baby and mother. Understanding the nuances of breastfeeding can make the journey more enjoyable and successful.

1. The Benefits of Breastfeeding

Breast milk is a complete and nutritionally balanced source of food for newborns. It contains essential nutrients that support their growth and development, including antibodies that protect them from infections. Breastfeeding also fosters a strong emotional bond between the mother and baby, thanks to the release of oxytocin during nursing sessions.

2. Establishing a Successful Breastfeeding Routine

Correct latching techniques are crucial for successful breastfeeding. Ensuring that your baby latches properly helps prevent sore nipples and ensures efficient milk transfer. It's essential to feed your baby on demand and recognize their hunger cues. Some babies may want to nurse more frequently, while others may nurse for longer durations. If breastfeeding is challenging, seeking support from lactation consultants or breastfeeding support groups can be immensely beneficial.

3. Expressing and Storing Breast Milk

If you need to be away from your baby or want to share feeding responsibilities with others, expressing breast milk is an option. Manual or electric breast pumps can help you express milk effectively. Proper storage and handling of breast milk are essential to maintain its nutritional value and safety for your baby.

4. Overcoming Breastfeeding Challenges

While breastfeeding is natural, it can be challenging for some mothers and babies. Engorgement, nipple pain, and difficulties with latch are common issues that can arise. Seeking assistance from a lactation consultant or attending breastfeeding support groups can help overcome these challenges and ensure successful breastfeeding.

Sleep Routines for Newborns

Sleep is crucial for a newborn's growth and development. Establishing healthy sleep routines helps your baby get the rest they need while providing you with essential rest as well.

1. Sleep Patterns in Newborns

Newborns sleep a lot, but their sleep is divided into shorter cycles of REM (Rapid Eye Movement) and non-REM sleep. Understanding your baby's sleep patterns can help you create a suitable sleep routine.

2. Sleep Environment

Creating a safe and conducive sleep environment is essential for your baby's well-being. The American Academy of Pediatrics (AAP) recommends placing your baby to sleep on their back in a crib with a firm mattress and without any soft bedding, toys, or pillows.

3. Creating a Sleep Routine

Consistency and predictability are key when establishing a sleep routine. Design a calming bedtime routine that signals to your baby that it's time to sleep. This may include activities like a warm bath, gentle massage, and reading a bedtime story.

4. Nighttime Sleep Strategies

Newborns may wake up frequently during the night for feeding and comfort. Responding promptly to their needs during nighttime awakenings helps them feel secure and reduces nighttime stress for both parents and baby.

5. Napping Schedule

Newborns need regular naps throughout the day to support their growth and development. Watch for signs of tiredness, such as rubbing eyes or yawning, and establish a consistent nap schedule to ensure your baby gets enough rest.

Handling Postpartum Challenges

The postpartum period (six to eight weeks after birth) can be physically and emotionally demanding for mothers. Understanding and addressing postpartum challenges is essential for a healthy recovery.

1. Physical Recovery and Self-Care

The postpartum body undergoes various changes, including hormonal fluctuations and physical healing. It's essential to listen to your body and give it time to recover. Engaging in light exercises, such as walking, can help improve mood and energy levels. Adequate nutrition and hydration are crucial, especially for breastfeeding mothers.

Postpartum depression and anxiety affect many new mothers. It's essential to recognize the signs and symptoms and seek help if needed. Talking openly about your feelings with your partner, family, or a healthcare professional can help you cope with these emotional challenges.

3. Partner Support and Communication

The postpartum period is a time of adjustment for both parents. Providing emotional support to each other and communicating openly about your needs and feelings can strengthen your relationship and make the transition to parenthood smoother.

Conclusion

The newborn stage is an incredible and transformative period for both parents and infants. Understanding the intricacies of caring for a newborn, establishing successful breastfeeding practices, implementing healthy sleep routines, and navigating postpartum challenges empowers parents to provide the best possible care for their little ones. With this comprehensive guide, you can embark on your parenting journey with confidence, love, and preparedness, ensuring a happy and thriving start for your precious bundle of joy.

Introduction

Nurturing infants is a critical aspect of child development and care. The first few years of life are crucial for forming strong bonds, developing communication skills, and meeting the emotional needs of infants. In this comprehensive guide, we will delve into the essential components of nurturing infants, exploring the significance of bonding, effective communication strategies, and methods to fulfill their emotional requirements.

The Importance of Bonding

Bonding is the foundation of a secure attachment between infants and their caregivers. It establishes the emotional connection necessary for healthy socio-emotional development. Here are some key aspects of bonding:

1. Skin-to-Skin Contact

Skin-to-skin contact is highly beneficial in the early stages of infancy. This practice, often referred to as "kangaroo care," helps regulate the baby's body temperature, heart rate, and breathing. Additionally, it promotes the release of oxytocin, a hormone that enhances the bonding process.

2. Eye Contact and Smiling

Engaging in eye contact and smiling at your infant can foster a sense of security and trust. Babies are drawn to facial expressions and gestures, which communicate love and affection.

3. Responsive Caregiving

Being responsive to an infant's needs, such as feeding, diaper changes, and comfort, reinforces the bond between the caregiver and the baby. Prompt and sensitive responses build the foundation for a secure attachment.

Effective Communication with Infants

While infants cannot yet verbalize their thoughts, they communicate through nonverbal cues and body language. Understanding and responding to these cues are essential for establishing effective communication. Here are some tips for effective communication with infants:

1. Active Listening

Even though infants do not speak, they communicate through coos, cries, and gestures. Actively listen and observe their cues to understand their needs and emotions.

2. Baby Talk and Infant-Directed Speech

Using baby talk or infant-directed speech, characterized by a higher pitch and simplified language, can engage infants and keep them attentive. This form of communication enhances their language development.

3. Mimicking and Imitation

Imitating your baby's sounds and facial expressions not only amuses them but also encourages reciprocity and social engagement. It is a vital aspect of early social communication development.

4. Gestures and Sign Language

Introducing simple gestures and sign language, such as waving goodbye or asking for "more," can facilitate communication before infants can speak verbally.

Meeting the Emotional Needs of Infants

Meeting the emotional needs of infants is essential for their overall well-being and lays the groundwork for future emotional regulation. Here are strategies to ensure these needs are fulfilled:

1. Emotional Availability

Caregivers must be emotionally available and attuned to the infant's emotional state. Responding to their emotions with sensitivity and empathy fosters emotional security.

2. Creating a Safe Environment

A safe and nurturing environment allows infants to explore and develop a sense of security. Ensure that their physical and emotional needs are met to create a stable and supportive atmosphere.

3. Routine and Predictability

Establishing consistent routines can provide infants with a sense of predictability, reducing anxiety and promoting emotional stability.

Separation anxiety is a common part of infant development. Gradual separation and reassurance during this phase help infants adapt to temporary separations from their primary caregivers.

Understanding Infant Developmental Milestones

Understanding infant developmental milestones is crucial for providing appropriate support and stimulation. While each baby develops at their pace, there are general milestones that can guide caregivers:

1. Cognitive Milestones

Cognitive development involves learning, problem-solving, and memory formation. Encourage exploration, provide age-appropriate toys, and engage in interactive play to stimulate cognitive growth.

2. Motor Milestones

Motor development includes both gross motor skills, like crawling and walking, and fine motor skills, like grasping objects. Create a safe environment that allows infants to explore and practice these skills.

3. Language Milestones

Language development involves babbling, understanding simple words, and eventually forming words and phrases. Engage in frequent verbal interactions, read books, and sing songs to support language acquisition.

Social and emotional milestones encompass developing attachment, recognizing emotions, and engaging in social interactions. Encourage positive social interactions and provide comfort during moments of distress.

Play and Sensory Stimulation

Play is a crucial aspect of infant development, promoting cognitive, motor, and socio-emotional growth. Additionally, sensory stimulation plays a vital role in early brain development. Here's how to enhance play and sensory experiences:

1. Tummy Time and Physical Play

Tummy time (period during the day baby spends awake and on their stomach) helps strengthen neck and back muscles, while physical play fosters gross motor skills. Engage in interactive play sessions and provide opportunities for physical exploration.

2. Sensory Toys and Activities

Offer a variety of sensory toys and activities that stimulate different senses, such as touch, sight, and sound. Sensory experiences support cognitive development and enhance neural connections.

3. Social Play and Interaction

Encourage social play by arranging playdates with other infants or participating in parent-infant classes. Social interactions contribute to emotional development and social skills.

Conclusion

Nurturing infants involves establishing strong bonds, effective communication, and fulfilling their emotional needs. The early years of life are vital for shaping a child's overall development and laying the groundwork for future growth. By being responsive, attentive, and supportive caregivers, we can create a nurturing environment that fosters healthy emotional and cognitive development in infants. Remember that every child is unique, and providing individualized care and attention will ensure their optimal growth and well-being.

Introduction to solid foods, balanced diets, and addressing picky eating

Introduction

Nutrition plays a crucial role in the overall growth and development of babies and toddlers. During the first few years of life, proper nutrition is essential to support their rapid physical and cognitive development. Introducing solid foods, providing balanced diets, and dealing with picky eating are key aspects that parents and caregivers should understand to ensure their child's health and well-being. This article will delve into the importance of healthy nutrition for babies and toddlers and offer practical tips to help parents navigate this critical phase of their child's life.

Introduction to Solid Foods

The introduction of solid foods is a major milestone in a baby's development, typically occurring around six months of age. Up until this point, breast milk or formula has been the primary source of nutrition. Introducing solid foods should be approached with care, as a baby's digestive system is still developing. Here are some essential guidelines for introducing solids:

1. Signs of Readiness

Before starting solids, observe your baby for signs of readiness. These may include:

> ➢ Ability to sit up with minimal support.

> Showing interest in food when others are eating.
> Loss of the tongue-thrust reflex (pushing food out of the mouth with the tongue).
> The ability to close lips around a spoon.

2. Start Slowly

When introducing solids, start with single-ingredient, easily digestible foods like rice cereal, pureed vegetables, or fruits. Give one new food at a time and wait for a few days before introducing another. This will help identify any potential allergies or intolerances.

3. Texture Progression

As your baby becomes comfortable with solid foods, gradually introduce thicker textures and small soft pieces to encourage chewing and development of oral motor skills.

Building a Balanced Diet

A balanced diet is crucial for ensuring that babies and toddlers receive the necessary nutrients for growth and development. As their nutritional needs change, it's essential to offer a variety of foods that provide a wide range of nutrients. Here are some guidelines for building a balanced diet:

1. Breast Milk or Formula

Breast milk or formula remains an essential part of a baby's diet until their first birthday. These provide essential nutrients and antibodies that support their immune system.

Once solid foods are introduced, aim to include a variety of fruits, vegetables, whole grains, lean proteins, and dairy (or dairy alternatives) in your child's diet. Gradually increase the variety of foods to expose them to different flavors and textures.

3. Nutrient-Rich Foods

Ensure that the diet includes nutrient-rich foods such as:

Iron-rich foods: Iron is crucial for brain development. Include iron-fortified cereals, lean meats, and legumes.

Omega-3 fatty acids: These support brain and eye development. Include fatty fish, flaxseeds, and chia seeds.

Calcium: Vital for bone development. Offer dairy or fortified plant-based milk products.

Vitamin D: Helps in calcium absorption. Expose your child to sunlight and consider a supplement if necessary.

4. Limit Sugary and Processed Foods

Minimize the intake of sugary and processed foods as they offer little nutritional value and can lead to unhealthy eating habits later in life.

Addressing Picky Eating

Picky eating is a common behavior among toddlers and can be frustrating for parents. However, it is a normal part of their development as they assert their independence and explore their preferences. Here are some strategies to address picky eating:

1. Be Patient and Persistent

Introducing new foods may take several attempts before a child accepts them. Be patient and persistent, offering the same food prepared in different ways.

2. Be a Role Model

Children often imitate their parents' eating habits. Set a good example by eating a variety of healthy foods yourself.

3. Involve Them in Meal Preparation

Let your child participate in age-appropriate ways during meal preparation. This involvement can make them more excited to try the food they helped prepare.

4. Serve Small Portions

Offer small portions of new foods to avoid overwhelming your child. Gradually increase the serving size if they show interest.

5. Avoid Using Food as a Reward or Punishment

Using food as a reward or punishment can create an unhealthy relationship with food. Instead, offer praise and encouragement for trying new foods.

Conclusion

Healthy nutrition is vital for the proper growth and development of babies and toddlers. The introduction of solid foods, providing a balanced diet, and addressing picky eating are essential aspects that parents and caregivers should focus on. By following these guidelines and being patient with the process, parents can ensure that their children develop healthy eating habits that will set them up for a lifetime of good health and well-being.

Introduction

The toddler years are a crucial and fascinating period in a child's development. It is a time when toddlers are rapidly growing, exploring their world, and learning new skills at an astonishing rate. This stage, typically spanning from 1 to 3 years of age, presents unique challenges and opportunities for parents and caregivers to support healthy development, encourage independence, and implement positive discipline techniques. In this comprehensive guide, we will delve into the various aspects of toddler development and provide practical tips to navigate this exciting phase with confidence and understanding.

Understanding Toddler Development

1. Physical Growth and Motor Skills

During the toddler years, children experience significant physical growth and refinement of motor skills. They become more adept at walking, running, climbing, and manipulating objects. Gross motor skills like balancing and coordination improve, enabling them to explore their environment more independently. Fine motor skills, such as picking up small objects and using utensils, also develop rapidly.

2. Language Development

Toddlers go through a language explosion during this stage. They begin to form words, use gestures to communicate, and gradually build their vocabulary. Language development is essential for expressing needs and emotions, fostering social interactions, and paving the way for further cognitive growth.

3. Cognitive Development

Toddlers are like sponges, absorbing information from their surroundings. Their cognitive development includes exploring cause-and-effect relationships, understanding simple concepts like size and quantity, and engaging in imaginative play. They are curious learners who eagerly explore the world around them.

4. Emotional and Social Development

Toddlers experience a wide range of emotions, from joy and excitement to frustration and tantrums. Developing emotional intelligence (ability to understand, manage, and express emotions effectively) during this phase is crucial for identifying and managing emotions effectively. Additionally, toddlers begin to engage in parallel play (play near each other but engage in independent activities) and simple interactions with peers, laying the foundation for future social skills.

Encouraging Independence

1. Creating a Safe Environment

Allowing toddlers to explore their surroundings independently is essential for fostering their sense of autonomy. However, it's crucial to create a safe and child-proofed environment to minimize potential hazards. This way, toddlers can explore freely without constant intervention.

2. Offering Choices

Providing toddlers with age-appropriate choices empowers them to assert their preferences and decisions. For instance, offering two outfit options or letting them choose between two snack options can encourage a sense of autonomy and independence.

3. Promoting Self-Help Skills

Encourage self-help skills by allowing toddlers to feed themselves, dress independently (even if it takes longer), and participate in simple chores like putting toys away. These activities build confidence and a sense of accomplishment.

4. Patience and Support

As toddlers strive for independence, they may encounter frustration and setbacks. Be patient and offer support when needed, allowing them to persevere through challenges and learn from their experiences.

Positive Discipline Techniques

1. Setting Clear Boundaries

Establishing clear and consistent boundaries helps toddlers understand acceptable behavior. Clearly communicate rules and expectations, and ensure that consequences for breaking rules are fair and age-appropriate.

2. Redirection

Redirecting a toddler's attention from an inappropriate behavior to a more acceptable activity is an effective way to prevent conflict and encourage positive behavior. For instance, if a toddler is playing with an off-limits object, gently direct their focus to a suitable toy.

3. Time-In instead of Time-Out

Rather than traditional time-outs, consider using time-ins, where you sit with your child and discuss their feelings and actions calmly. This approach fosters emotional connection and understanding, helping toddlers learn from their mistakes and develop empathy.

4. Positive Reinforcement

Acknowledging and praising positive behavior reinforces it and encourages its repetition. Celebrate small achievements and efforts, which boosts a toddler's self-esteem and encourages positive behavior.

Conclusion

The toddler years are an exciting time of growth and development. Understanding toddler development, encouraging independence, and implementing positive discipline techniques are essential for supporting their journey toward becoming confident, capable individuals. As parents and caregivers, being attuned to their needs, providing a safe environment, and fostering a nurturing atmosphere will help toddlers thrive during this significant phase of their lives. Embrace the challenges, cherish the milestones, and enjoy the precious moments of the toddler years, for they are the building blocks of a lifetime.

Introduction

Play is an essential aspect of a child's development, serving as a fundamental building block for their physical, cognitive, emotional, and social growth. Through play, children explore the world around them, discover their capabilities, and develop critical skills that lay the foundation for future learning and success. This article will delve into the significance of play in a child's development and explore age-appropriate activities that can support their growth in various stages of childhood.

The Role of Play in Child Development

1. Cognitive Development

Play serves as a natural way for children to engage their minds, encouraging curiosity and imagination. During play, children problem-solve, make decisions, and learn to think creatively. For instance, building with blocks fosters spatial awareness and logical reasoning, while pretend play helps develop symbolic thinking and storytelling abilities. The freedom to experiment and learn from mistakes in play enhances a child's cognitive flexibility and adaptability.

2. Physical Development

Physical play is crucial for a child's motor skill development. Activities such as running, jumping, climbing, and playing sports contribute to the growth of gross motor skills, promoting strength, balance, and coordination. Fine motor skills are refined through activities like drawing, cutting, and manipulating small objects, which are essential for tasks like writing and using tools.

3. Emotional Development

Play provides an emotional outlet for children, allowing them to express and process their feelings in a safe and imaginative manner. Pretend play (act out fictional scenarios and take on roles, often imitating real-life situations or characters), for example, enables children to role-play different scenarios, which helps them understand and cope with various emotions. Furthermore, social play interactions teach empathy, cooperation, and emotional regulation, as children learn to navigate conflicts and negotiate with others.

4. Social Development

Playtime is an opportunity for children to interact with peers, family members, and caregivers, which is vital for their social development. Through play, children learn essential social skills such as sharing, taking turns, and communication. Cooperative games, group activities, and pretend play foster teamwork and collaboration, contributing to the development of healthy relationships and a sense of belonging.

The Power of Age-Appropriate Play

1. Infants (0-12 months)

During infancy, play primarily involves sensory exploration and establishing bonds with caregivers. Simple activities like peek-a-boo (one person hides their face or body and then reveals themselves), rattles (handheld toys typically made of a container filled with small objects like beads or small pellets, produce a rattling sound when shaken), and tummy time aid in developing the baby's senses and motor skills. Engaging in nurturing and responsive interactions during play helps build trust and a sense of security.

2. Toddlers (1-3 years)

Toddlers are curious explorers who benefit from play that encourages physical movement, language development, and imaginative thinking. Activities like stacking blocks, playing with shape sorters, and engaging in pretend play with dolls or toy cars promote fine motor skills and language acquisition. Outdoor play, such as swinging and sliding, enhances gross motor skills and offers opportunities for social interaction.

3. Preschoolers (3-5 years)

Preschoolers' play becomes more imaginative and complex. Art activities like drawing and finger painting foster creativity, while building with construction toys enhances problem-solving and spatial skills. Pretend play with dress-up costumes and role-playing scenarios allows them to make sense of the world around them and practice social roles.

4. Early School Age (6-8 years)

At this stage, children enjoy games with rules and structured play. Board games, team sports, and interactive video games encourage strategic thinking, cooperation, and healthy competition. Art and craft activities that require more intricate designs promote fine motor skills and attention to detail.

5. Middle Childhood (9-12 years)

During middle childhood, play can involve more complex tasks and hobbies that align with their interests. Building models, participating in team sports, and engaging in creative writing or storytelling support cognitive and social development. Playtime continues to be crucial for stress relief and emotional well-being during this transitional phase.

Balancing Structured Learning and Play

While structured learning is essential for academic growth, it's equally important to maintain a balance between formal education and playtime. Play complements formal learning by reinforcing concepts, fostering a love for learning, and allowing children to apply academic knowledge in real-life scenarios. Moreover, play encourages self-directed learning and problem-solving, empowering children to become lifelong learners.

Creating a Play-Conducive Environment

1. At Home

Parents can create a play-conducive environment at home by providing a variety of age-appropriate toys, art supplies, and books. Designating a dedicated play area and allowing ample unstructured playtime encourages children to explore their interests freely. Parents should actively participate in play and demonstrate enthusiasm, as their involvement fosters deeper engagement and bonding.

Educators play a vital role in facilitating play-based learning in schools. Incorporating play into the curriculum through educational games, interactive activities, and hands-on projects supports students' learning and motivation. Outdoor play areas and recess breaks provide children with opportunities for physical activity, social interaction, and stress release.

Nurturing Playfulness for Lifelong Learning

Play is not confined to childhood; its positive impact extends throughout life. Encouraging a playful attitude in adults promotes creativity, problem-solving, and stress reduction. In the workplace, incorporating playful elements can foster a more productive and collaborative environment. As adults, we can lead by example, embracing playfulness in our lives and showing children that learning is an exciting and continuous journey.

Conclusion

Playtime holds immense significance in a child's development, providing a platform for holistic growth across cognitive, physical, emotional, and social domains. Age-appropriate play activities tailored to each developmental stage are instrumental in nurturing a child's potential and creating a strong foundation for lifelong learning. By recognizing and promoting the power of play, parents, educators, and caregivers can play a pivotal role in supporting children's well-being and academic success.

Introduction

Preschool is an exciting milestone in a child's life that marks the beginning of their formal education journey. It is a critical time for children to develop essential skills, socialize with peers, and foster a love for learning. However, starting preschool can also be a challenging experience for both children and parents. In this comprehensive guide, we will explore how to prepare your child for preschool, the importance of socialization during this phase, and how to support your child's early learning journey.

Preparing for Preschool

1. Understanding the Benefits of Preschool

Preschool provides numerous benefits for children, setting a strong foundation for their academic, social, and emotional growth. Research has shown that children who attend preschool are more likely to develop stronger language and math skills, better attention spans, and improved self-regulation abilities. Moreover, the early exposure to structured learning environments enhances their readiness for kindergarten and beyond.

2. Choosing the Right Preschool

Selecting the right preschool for your child is crucial to ensure they have a positive and enriching experience.

Consider factors such as location, curriculum, teacher-to-student ratio, safety measures, and the school's philosophy on early childhood education. Visiting the preschools, talking to teachers, and seeking recommendations from other parents can help you make an informed decision.

3. Gradual Familiarization

Before the first day of preschool, gradually introduce your child to the idea of school. Talk about what they can expect, read books about starting preschool, and visit the school together if possible. Creating a sense of familiarity can help alleviate anxiety and make the transition smoother for your child.

4. Establishing a Routine

Preschool introduces a structured routine, which can differ significantly from a child's daily life at home. To prepare your child, establish a consistent daily routine that includes designated playtime, learning time, and nap time. This will help your child adjust to the structure they will encounter at preschool.

5. Developing Independence Skills

Preschool requires children to be more independent in various tasks, such as using the restroom, dressing themselves, and tidying up after playtime. Encourage and support your child in developing these essential self-help skills to boost their confidence and self-reliance.

6. Managing Separation Anxiety

Separation anxiety is a common concern when starting preschool. Practice brief separations from your child before the first day of school to help them cope with being away from you. Assure them that you will always come back and that preschool will be a fun place to learn and make new friends.

The Importance of Socialization

1. Learning Through Play and Peer Interaction

Socialization in preschool plays a vital role in a child's development. Through play and interacting with peers, children learn important social skills such as sharing, taking turns, cooperation, empathy, and conflict resolution. These skills are essential for building positive relationships in the future.

2. Enhancing Communication Skills

Interacting with peers and teachers at preschool provides children with ample opportunities to practice and improve their communication skills. They learn to express themselves, ask questions, and listen to others, which are fundamental skills that extend beyond the preschool years.

3. Fostering Emotional Development

Preschool allows children to experience a wide range of emotions in a safe and supportive environment. They learn to identify their feelings, manage emotions, and develop emotional intelligence, all of which contribute to their overall well-being and mental health.

4. Cultivating Empathy and Understanding Differences

In a diverse preschool setting, children encounter peers from various backgrounds and cultures. This exposure fosters empathy and a sense of understanding and appreciation for differences, promoting a more inclusive and compassionate society.

5. Building Confidence and Self-Esteem

Positive interactions with peers and successful social experiences at preschool can boost a child's confidence and self-esteem. Feeling accepted and valued by their peers and teachers reinforces a positive self-image.

Supporting Early Learning

1. Play-Based Learning

Preschool curriculum often revolves around play-based learning, where children engage in activities that are both fun and educational. Play allows children to explore, experiment, and develop problem-solving skills while fostering a love for learning.

2. Encouraging Curiosity and Exploration

Preschool is a time when children are naturally curious about the world around them. Encourage their inquisitiveness by answering their questions, providing age-appropriate learning materials, and engaging them in hands-on activities.

3. Reading Together

Reading is a powerful tool for early learning. Establish a daily reading routine with your child, exploring a variety of books to expand their vocabulary, stimulate imagination, and strengthen cognitive skills.

4. Incorporating Learning into Daily Activities

Learning doesn't have to be limited to the preschool setting. Find opportunities to incorporate learning into everyday activities, such as counting during playtime, discussing shapes during mealtime, or identifying colors during outdoor walks.

5. Nurturing Creativity and Imagination

Preschool is a time when creativity and imagination soar. Provide art supplies, encourage imaginative play, and praise their creativity to nurture their artistic and innovative abilities.

6. Celebrating Effort and Progress

Acknowledge and celebrate your child's efforts and progress in their early learning journey. Positive reinforcement and encouragement can fuel their motivation to explore, learn, and overcome challenges.

Conclusion

Starting preschool is a significant milestone for children and their families. By preparing your child for preschool, understanding the importance of socialization, and actively supporting their early learning journey, you can lay a strong foundation for their academic and personal growth. Remember that each child is unique, and the preschool experience will vary for everyone. Be patient, stay involved, and celebrate the joy of learning together as your child embarks on this exciting educational adventure.

Introduction

Language development is a critical aspect of a child's growth and plays a vital role in their overall cognitive, emotional, and social development. From birth to early childhood, children go through a remarkable process of learning and acquiring language skills. As parents, caregivers, and educators, it is essential to understand the various stages of language development and employ effective strategies to support and enhance a child's language abilities. This article aims to provide a comprehensive guide to fostering language skills and addressing speech delays if any, for the well-rounded development of a child.

The Stages of Language Development

1. Prelinguistic Stage (0-12 months)

During this stage, infants engage in nonverbal communication, such as cooing, crying, babbling, and gestures. They develop an understanding of facial expressions, tone of voice, and body language to communicate their needs and emotions.

2. Babbling Stage (6-12 months)

Babbling marks the beginning of language development. Babies produce repetitive syllables, like "ba-ba" or "da-da," experimenting with various sounds. This stage lays the foundation for speech development as infants start mimicking the sounds they hear.

3. One-Word Stage (12-18 months)

Toddlers begin uttering their first recognizable words, typically referring to important people, objects, or actions in their environment. They learn new words rapidly during this phase and gradually start understanding simple instructions.

4. Two-Word Stage (18-24 months)

In this phase, children combine two words to form simple phrases, such as "more milk" or "big ball." They show increasing comprehension of basic grammar rules and build their vocabulary through daily interactions.

5. Early Language Development (2-3 years)

Children's language skills expand rapidly during this period. They form longer sentences, use pronouns, and ask questions to satisfy their curiosity about the world. Vocabulary growth continues, allowing them to express their thoughts and feelings more comprehensively.

6. Language Refinement (3-5 years)

At this stage, language development becomes more sophisticated. Children use more complex sentence structures and show better control over grammar and syntax. Their storytelling abilities and imaginative play flourish during this period.

Tips for Fostering Language Skills

1. Encourage Responsive Communication

Engage in responsive communication with your child from infancy. Respond to their coos, babbling, and gestures to let them know their communication attempts are acknowledged. Maintain eye contact and use facial expressions to convey emotions effectively.

2. Read Aloud Regularly

Reading aloud to children promotes language development and a love for books. Choose age-appropriate books with colorful illustrations, rhythmic patterns, and engaging stories. Encourage children to participate by asking questions and discussing the plot.

3. Engage in Conversations

Hold regular conversations with your child, even if they can't respond fluently. Narrate daily activities, describe objects, and encourage them to respond through gestures or vocalizations. This back-and-forth exchange boosts language comprehension and vocabulary.

4. Create a Language-Rich Environment

Expose children to a language-rich environment by playing educational games, listening to music, and watching age-appropriate shows. Use descriptive language and encourage discussions about their experiences and observations.

5. Use Visual Aids and Sign Language

Incorporate visual aids, such as flashcards and picture books, to reinforce vocabulary. Additionally, teaching basic sign language can help bridge communication gaps for children with speech delays and enhance language skills for all children.

6. Foster Social Interactions

Encourage your child to interact with peers and adults in various settings, like playdates or group activities. Social interactions provide opportunities for language practice and help children understand different communication styles.

7. Limit Screen Time

Excessive screen time can hinder language development. Set limits on screen usage and prioritize face-to-face interactions and real-life experiences to foster language skills.

Addressing Speech Delays

1. Early Intervention is Key

If you notice any concerns regarding your child's language development or speech delays, seek professional evaluation and early intervention services. Early identification and intervention significantly improve outcomes for children with speech delays.

2. Consult a Speech-Language Pathologist

A speech-language pathologist (SLP) is a trained professional who can assess and provide targeted therapy for speech delays. They can design personalized interventions to address specific language difficulties.

3. Provide a Supportive Environment

Create a supportive and non-judgmental environment for your child. Avoid interrupting or finishing their sentences, as it may discourage them from communicating. Be patient and give them ample time to express themselves.

4. Practice Speech Exercises at Home

Work with the SLP to practice speech exercises at home. Consistency is crucial for progress, so dedicate time daily to reinforce what your child is learning in therapy.

5. Encourage Peer Interaction

Encourage your child to interact with peers who have age-appropriate language skills. Positive peer influence can motivate them to practice communication and build their confidence.

6. Celebrate Progress

Celebrate every achievement, no matter how small. Positive reinforcement and praise can boost a child's confidence and encourage continued effort.

Conclusion

Language development is a dynamic and fascinating journey in a child's life. As parents and caregivers, fostering language skills and addressing speech delays require patience, understanding, and dedication. By creating a language-rich environment, engaging in responsive communication, and seeking timely intervention when needed, we can empower children to communicate effectively and confidently, unlocking their full potential for lifelong success and fulfillment.

Introduction

Emotional intelligence plays a crucial role in a child's overall development and well-being. As children grow and navigate the complexities of life, it is essential for caregivers, parents, and educators to promote emotional intelligence early on. This article explores the importance of emotional intelligence in child development and offers practical strategies to help children identify and manage their emotions effectively.

Understanding Emotional Intelligence in Children

Emotional intelligence refers to a person's ability to recognize, understand, and manage their own emotions, as well as empathize with the emotions of others. In children, emotional intelligence lays the foundation for healthy social relationships, improved communication, and better academic performance. Developing emotional intelligence from an early age can lead to more emotionally resilient and empathetic individuals in adulthood.

The Role of Caregivers and Parents in Promoting Emotional Intelligence

Children learn emotional intelligence primarily through observation and interactions with their caregivers and parents. Therefore, it is essential for adults to model healthy emotional expression and provide a supportive environment for children to express their feelings openly. When parents and caregivers demonstrate empathy, active listening, and emotional regulation, children are more likely to internalize these skills.

Creating an Emotionally Safe Environment

To foster emotional intelligence, it is crucial to establish an emotionally safe environment for children. This involves validating their emotions, avoiding judgmental responses, and encouraging open communication. When children feel safe expressing their feelings, they are more likely to develop a healthy understanding of their emotions and learn how to manage them effectively.

Teaching Emotional Vocabulary

One of the fundamental aspects of emotional intelligence is the ability to identify and label emotions accurately. Caregivers and educators can help children develop emotional vocabulary by explicitly teaching them different emotions and their corresponding expressions. Engaging in conversations about emotions and encouraging children to articulate their feelings enhances their emotional literacy.

Encouraging Emotional Expression

Children need to know that it is okay to express a wide range of emotions. Encouraging emotional expression, whether positive or negative, helps children feel understood and validated. As caregivers, we can teach children healthy ways to express emotions through art, storytelling, journaling, or simply talking about how they feel.

Practicing Mindfulness and Emotional Awareness

Mindfulness practices can significantly contribute to the development of emotional intelligence. Teaching children to be present in the moment and to observe their thoughts and emotions without judgment cultivates emotional awareness. Mindfulness exercises such as deep breathing and body scans can be integrated into daily routines to help children regulate their emotions effectively.

Building Empathy and Perspective-Taking

Empathy is a cornerstone of emotional intelligence. By helping children understand the feelings and perspectives of others, we foster their ability to empathize and connect with those around them. Storytelling, role-playing, and group discussions are effective tools for promoting empathy in children.

Problem-Solving and Conflict Resolution

Emotional intelligence involves being able to manage emotions during conflicts and problem-solving situations. Caregivers can guide children in developing healthy conflict resolution skills, such as active listening, compromise, and seeking win-win solutions. These skills not only enhance emotional intelligence but also contribute to the development of strong interpersonal relationships.

Encouraging Emotional Regulation

Emotional regulation is the ability to manage and control one's emotions effectively. Children need guidance in identifying their emotional triggers and adopting coping strategies when facing challenging situations. Deep breathing exercises, counting to ten, or taking a short break are some practical techniques that can help children regulate their emotions.

Practicing Emotional Intelligence through Play

Play is an integral part of a child's development, and it can be used as a tool to promote emotional intelligence. Through pretend play and storytelling, children can explore various emotions and scenarios, allowing them to practice emotional regulation and empathy in a safe and enjoyable setting.

Conclusion

Promoting emotional intelligence in children is an investment in their future well-being and success. As caregivers, parents, and educators, our role in nurturing emotional intelligence is vital. By creating an emotionally safe environment, teaching emotional vocabulary, encouraging expression, and practicing mindfulness, empathy, and problem-solving, we equip children with essential skills to navigate life's challenges with resilience and compassion. Emphasizing emotional intelligence in child development ensures that we raise emotionally intelligent individuals who can thrive in a complex and interconnected world.

Introduction

Discipline and boundaries play a crucial role in a child's development and care. As children grow and explore the world around them, they require guidance and structure to learn appropriate behaviors, develop self-control, and cultivate a sense of responsibility. In this comprehensive guide, we will delve into the importance of discipline and setting boundaries with empathy, exploring effective strategies that foster a positive and nurturing environment for children to flourish.

Understanding the Role of Discipline in Child Development

Discipline is not synonymous with punishment; rather, it is about teaching and guiding children to make responsible decisions. When approached with empathy, discipline serves as a powerful tool to instill values, morals, and good behavior in children. Effective discipline lays the foundation for healthy emotional and social development.

The Science Behind Boundaries

Boundaries are like the fences that protect a child's physical and emotional space. Research in child psychology suggests that children thrive when they have clear, consistent, and age-appropriate boundaries. Boundaries provide a sense of security, enabling children to explore and learn within a structured framework.

The Role of Parents and Caregivers in Establishing Boundaries

Parents and caregivers play a vital role in establishing and enforcing boundaries. They need to act as role models, demonstrating respect and understanding while setting limits. By maintaining a balance between warmth and authority, parents can create a supportive environment where children feel safe to express themselves and make mistakes.

Setting Age-Appropriate Boundaries

Age-appropriate boundaries evolve as children grow and develop. Infants and toddlers require physical safety boundaries, while preschoolers benefit from consistent routines and clear expectations. As children enter their school years, emotional boundaries become essential, promoting healthy communication and conflict resolution.

Empathy as the Key to Effective Discipline

Empathy is the cornerstone of successful discipline. Understanding a child's feelings and perspective allows parents and caregivers to respond compassionately to challenging behaviors. Instead of reacting impulsively, empathetic discipline focuses on teaching children about emotions and appropriate ways to express them.

Positive Reinforcement and Rewards

Positive reinforcement is a powerful discipline tool that emphasizes praising and rewarding desired behaviors. Celebrating a child's achievements and efforts reinforces positive conduct and encourages them to make better choices. This approach builds self-esteem and confidence, leading to a stronger sense of self-worth.

Natural Consequences vs. Punishment

When children make mistakes, it's essential for them to experience natural consequences. Unlike punishment, which aims to inflict pain or discomfort, natural consequences allow children to learn from their actions. For example, if a child refuses to eat dinner, the natural consequence may be feeling hungry later in the evening. However, it is crucial for parents and caregivers to ensure that natural consequences are safe and age-appropriate.

Time-Outs and Cooling-Off Periods

Time-outs can be effective in giving children a chance to calm down and reflect on their behavior. When used with empathy, time-outs become an opportunity for children to learn self-regulation and develop problem-solving skills. Creating a designated space for time-outs and discussing feelings afterward fosters emotional intelligence.

The Art of Redirection

Redirection is a gentle discipline strategy that involves diverting a child's attention from inappropriate behavior to a more acceptable activity. This approach works well, particularly with young children, and helps them learn what is acceptable in various situations.

Consistency and Predictability

Consistency is paramount in discipline and boundary-setting. Children thrive in environments where rules are predictable and enforced uniformly. When parents and caregivers are consistent, children learn to trust and feel secure in their surroundings.

Communicating Boundaries Effectively

Clear and open communication is vital when establishing boundaries. Parents and caregivers should communicate the reasons behind rules and boundaries, enabling children to understand the logic and purpose behind them. Discussions about boundaries should occur calmly and respectfully, encouraging children to express their thoughts and concerns.

Flexibility and Adjusting Boundaries

While consistency is essential, it's also crucial to remain flexible in certain situations. As children grow and change, some boundaries may need adjustment to suit their developmental needs and capabilities. Adapting boundaries with empathy demonstrates that parents are attentive to their child's growth and development.

Empowering Children through Choice

Providing children with age-appropriate choices empowers them to take responsibility for their actions. Offering limited options allows children to feel in control of their decisions while still operating within established boundaries.

Modeling Boundaries in Digital Spaces

In the digital age, it is crucial to establish boundaries around screen time and online activities. Modeling healthy behaviors and setting boundaries around technology use helps children develop responsible digital habits and navigate online spaces safely.

Recognizing Individual Differences

Each child is unique, and what works for one may not work for another. It is essential to recognize and respect individual differences when establishing discipline strategies and setting boundaries. Tailoring approaches to a child's personality and temperament enhances their receptiveness to discipline and promotes a positive parent-child relationship.

Conclusion

Discipline and boundaries, when implemented with empathy, are essential aspects of child development and care. By understanding the role of discipline, the science behind boundaries, and the importance of empathy, parents and caregivers can foster a nurturing environment that promotes healthy emotional, social, and behavioral growth in children. Establishing effective discipline strategies and setting boundaries with empathy paves the way for resilient, responsible, and well-adjusted individuals who can thrive in an ever-changing world.

Introduction

Creativity and imagination are fundamental aspects of a child's cognitive and emotional development. Nurturing these qualities from a young age can have a profound impact on a child's overall growth and future success. In this article, we will explore various strategies and activities to encourage creativity and artistic expression in children. By fostering a creative environment, parents, caregivers, and educators can help children unleash their imaginations and reach their full potential.

Create an Inspiring Environment

One of the first steps in encouraging creativity in children is to create an inspiring environment. Surround them with diverse materials, colors, and shapes that stimulate their senses and curiosity. Provide ample space for them to explore and experiment freely. A dedicated arts and crafts corner or a storytelling nook can be excellent additions to your child's play area.

Embrace Open-Ended Play

Open-ended play (no specific rules or predetermined outcomes, allowing children to explore and create freely with toys and materials) allows children to explore their imaginations without predefined outcomes. Encourage them to engage in activities such as building blocks, drawing, painting, and pretend play. Avoid imposing strict rules or templates, as this may stifle their creativity. Instead, let them create their own narratives and unique expressions.

Foster Curiosity through Storytelling

Storytelling is a powerful tool to spark imagination in children. Read them a variety of stories, including fairytales, folktales, and books with fantastical elements. Encourage them to create their own stories by asking questions about characters, settings, and plots. This exercise will help them develop their narrative skills and imaginative thinking.

Encourage Artistic Expression

Art is a wonderful medium for children to express their thoughts, feelings, and dreams. Provide them with art supplies like crayons, colored pencils, paints, and clay to experiment with different forms of expression. Celebrate their artistic endeavors by displaying their artwork around the house or creating a family art gallery.

Support Role-Play and Dress-Up

Role-playing and dress-up games enable children to step into different roles and explore various scenarios. Encourage them to dress up as their favorite characters or pretend to be professionals like doctors, chefs, or astronauts. This form of play enhances their creativity and helps them understand different perspectives.

Incorporate Music and Dance

Music and dance are powerful tools to ignite creativity in children. Play different genres of music and encourage them to move and dance freely. Provide musical instruments for them to explore, fostering their rhythmic abilities. Singing and dancing not only promote creativity but also aid in emotional expression and self-confidence.

Engage in Nature Exploration

Nature provides an endless source of inspiration for creativity. Take your child on nature walks, explore gardens, or visit parks. Encourage them to observe the beauty of plants, animals, and the changing seasons. Engaging with nature will trigger their imaginative minds and stimulate artistic ideas.

Introduce Creative Challenges

Present your child with creative challenges that push their boundaries. Offer age-appropriate puzzles, brain teasers, and art projects that encourage problem-solving and out-of-the-box thinking. Emphasize the process rather than the end result, as it is through experimentation that true creativity flourishes.

Encourage Collaboration and Group Activities

Group activities promote social interaction and collaboration, which can lead to creative synergy. Organize group art projects, drama performances, or storytelling sessions where children can work together and inspire one another. This fosters teamwork and exposes them to different perspectives, enriching their creative experiences.

Limit Screen Time

While technology has its benefits, excessive screen time can hinder creativity and imagination. Set reasonable limits on electronic devices and encourage other forms of play that involve hands-on exploration and interaction with the real world.

Conclusion

Encouraging creativity and imagination in children is a journey that requires patience, support, and a nurturing environment. By providing opportunities for open-ended play, artistic expression, storytelling, and nature exploration, we can help children unlock their full creative potential. Embrace their uniqueness, celebrate their ideas, and watch as their creativity flourishes, paving the way for a bright and imaginative future. As parents, caregivers, and educators, our role is to inspire and guide them on this creative adventure, for it is through their creativity that they will shape the world around them and leave a lasting impact on society.

Introduction

Sleep is an integral part of a child's development and overall well-being. It plays a crucial role in physical growth, cognitive development, emotional regulation, and immune function. As parents, caregivers, and educators, it is our responsibility to establish healthy sleep habits for children to promote their optimal growth and ensure they wake up refreshed and ready for the day ahead. In this article, we will delve into the importance of sleep routines, common sleep issues in children, and provide tips for a smooth transition to a big kid's bed.

The Significance of Sleep Routines for Children

1. Understanding the Circadian Rhythm

The circadian rhythm, often referred to as the "body clock," regulates the sleep-wake cycles in children. It synchronizes with external cues like sunlight and darkness, helping establish regular sleep patterns. Maintaining consistent sleep schedules is essential to support the body's natural rhythm, which contributes to better sleep quality and overall health.

2. Benefits of Sleep Routines

Having a structured sleep routine offers numerous advantages for children:

Improved Sleep Quality and Duration: Consistent bedtime and wake-up times help regulate the sleep-wake cycle, leading to more restful and rejuvenating sleep.

Enhanced Mood and Behavior: Well-rested children are generally happier, more focused, and less prone to behavioral issues.

Development of Self-Soothing Skills: A predictable bedtime routine enables children to learn self-soothing techniques, reducing the need for external sleep aids.

Strengthened Parent-Child Bonding: Bedtime routines provide valuable opportunities for parents to connect with their children on an emotional level, fostering a sense of security and trust.

3. Creating a Bedtime Routine

To establish an effective bedtime routine, consider the following steps:

Establishing a Consistent Bedtime: Determine an appropriate bedtime that allows for adequate sleep duration based on your child's age and individual needs. Stick to this schedule on weekdays and weekends to maintain a stable sleep pattern.

Calming Activities before Sleep: Engage in calming activities before bedtime, such as reading a bedtime story, listening to soft music, or practicing relaxation exercises.

The Role of Bedtime Stories and Lullabies: Bedtime stories and lullabies (soothing and gentle songs typically sung to infants and young children to help them fall asleep) have a soothing effect on children, helping them relax and transition to sleep more easily.

Addressing Common Sleep Issues in Children

1. Nighttime Fears and Nightmares

It is common for children to experience nighttime fears and occasional nightmares. Understanding the difference between the two is crucial for providing appropriate support:

Nighttime Fears: These are generally mild and transient fears that may include fear of the dark, imaginary creatures, or monsters. Offer comfort and reassurance, and use a nightlight if necessary.

Nightmares: Nightmares (distressing and vividly unpleasant dreams that often occur during the rapid eye movement stage of sleep) can be more intense and disruptive, leading to fear of sleeping. Comfort your child after a nightmare, validate their feelings, and assure them that bad dreams are not real.

2. Sleepwalking and Night Terrors

Sleepwalking and night terrors are different sleep disturbances that may occur in children:

Sleepwalking: Sleepwalking usually occurs during deep sleep stages and involves walking or performing other activities while asleep. Ensure a safe sleep environment by removing any hazards that could pose a risk during sleepwalking episodes.

: **Night terrors** (episodes of intense fear and distress that occur during non-REM sleep, usually in the first few hours after falling asleep) are characterized by sudden and intense fear, often accompanied by crying, screaming, or thrashing. Stay calm, ensure your child's safety, and avoid waking them during a night terror episode.

3. Bedtime Resistance and Sleep Delay

Bedtime resistance and sleep delay can be frustrating for parents, but understanding potential causes and employing appropriate strategies can help:

Identifying Potential Causes: Bedtime resistance may arise due to anxiety, overstimulation, or a desire for attention. Identifying the underlying cause is essential in addressing the issue effectively.

Strategies for Dealing with Bedtime Struggles: Create a consistent and calming bedtime routine, set clear expectations about bedtime, and avoid stimulating activities close to bedtime.

Promoting a Positive Sleep Environment: Ensure your child's bedroom is conducive to sleep by keeping it dark, quiet, and comfortable.

4. Sleep Regression

Sleep regression refers to periods when a previously good sleeper experiences disrupted sleep patterns:

Common Triggers: Sleep regression can be triggered by developmental milestones (specific skills, behaviors, or abilities that children typically achieve within certain age ranges), changes in routine, or external stressors.

: Stay patient during sleep regression phases, maintain consistent routines, and provide extra comfort and reassurance.

: Support your child through the regression phase by offering a familiar sleep environment and extra comfort during times of distress.

Transitioning to a Big Kid's Bed

1. Recognizing the Right Time for Transition

Transitioning to a big kid's bed is a significant milestone, but it is essential to recognize when your child is ready:

Signs of Readiness: Look for signs such as climbing out of the crib, expressing discomfort in the crib, or showing interest in a big bed.

Avoiding Premature Transitions: Moving your child too early may result in sleep disruptions and bedtime struggles.

2. Involving the Child in the Process

Engage your child in the transition process to make them feel excited and empowered:

Empowering the Child: Let your child choose their new bedding, pillows, or stuffed animals to make the new bed feel special.

3. Preparing the Bedroom

Ensure the bedroom is safe and inviting for your child's transition to a big kid's bed:

Safety-Proofing: Remove any potential hazards from the room and secure furniture to prevent accidents.

Creating a Cozy Environment: Make the new bed inviting with familiar items like their favorite blanket or stuffed animals.

4. Dealing with Sleep Regression During Transition

Be prepared for potential sleep disruptions during the transition:

Understanding the Possibility of Sleep Disruption: It is normal for children to experience sleep regression during significant changes like transitioning to a big bed.

Staying Patient and Consistent: Stick to the bedtime routine, offer comfort, and be patient as your child adjusts to the new sleep environment.

5. Nighttime Support and Reassurance

Support your child during the adjustment period to their new bed:

Responsive Parenting: Be attentive to your child's needs and provide comfort and reassurance as they adapt to the change.

: **Encourage your child to express their feelings and talk about their experience with the new bed.**

The Role of Technology in Healthy Sleep Habits

1. Screen Time and Sleep

Limiting screen time before bedtime is crucial for promoting healthy sleep:

Impact on Sleep Quality: **Electronic devices emit blue light that can interfere with the production of melatonin, a hormone that regulates sleep.**

Establishing Screen Time Rules: **Set clear boundaries on device use before bedtime to allow your child's body to prepare for sleep naturally.**

2. Utilizing Sleep Tracking Apps

Sleep tracking apps can be helpful but should be used with caution:

Pros and Cons: **Sleep tracking apps can provide valuable insights into your child's sleep patterns, but they should not replace professional evaluation if sleep issues persist.**

Best Practices: **Use sleep tracking apps as a tool for monitoring sleep patterns and identifying any potential issues.**

Conclusion

Establishing healthy sleep habits for children is a critical aspect of their overall well-being and development. A consistent bedtime routine offers numerous benefits, including improved sleep quality, enhanced mood, and stronger parent-child bonds. Addressing common sleep issues with patience and understanding is essential to support children through various challenges they may encounter during their sleep journey. Transitioning to a big kid's bed is an exciting milestone that can be facilitated by empowering the child and creating a safe and cozy sleep environment. By prioritizing healthy sleep habits and minimizing screen time, parents and caregivers play a pivotal role in fostering their child's optimal growth, development, and overall happiness.

Introduction

Ensuring the physical health and well-being of children is essential for their overall development and growth. As parents, caregivers, and educators, it is our responsibility to create an environment that promotes an active lifestyle, addresses common childhood illnesses, and instills healthy habits from a young age. This article will provide a comprehensive guide to nurturing physical health in children, offering practical tips and advice for a happy and healthy childhood.

Keeping Children Active

1. Importance of Physical Activity

Physical activity is crucial for children's physical, mental, and emotional development. It aids in the development of strong muscles and bones, improves cardiovascular health, and enhances motor skills. Regular physical activity also helps in maintaining a healthy body weight and reduces the risk of chronic diseases later in life.

2. Encouraging Play and Outdoor Activities

Children love to play, and playtime provides an excellent opportunity for them to be physically active. Encourage outdoor activities like running, jumping, cycling, and playing team sports. Outdoor play not only promotes physical health but also enhances social skills and creativity.

3. Limiting Screen Time

Excessive screen time, including television, smartphones, and tablets, can lead to a sedentary lifestyle. Set reasonable limits on screen time and prioritize physical activities instead. Engage children in interactive games, puzzles, and crafts to reduce their dependence on screens.

4. Family Physical Activities

Make physical activities a family affair. Plan regular outings such as hiking, swimming, or playing sports together. Family activities not only promote fitness but also create bonding moments and cherished memories.

5. Active Transportation

Encourage walking or cycling to nearby destinations instead of driving. Active transportation not only adds to children's daily physical activity but also promotes a sense of independence and responsibility.

Dealing with Common Illnesses

1. Building a Strong Immune System

A robust immune system is essential for protecting children from common illnesses. Ensure they follow a balanced diet that includes fruits, vegetables, whole grains, and proteins. Adequate sleep and regular exercise also play a crucial role in building a strong immune system.

2. Preventing Respiratory Infections

Respiratory infections like the common cold and flu are prevalent among children. Teach children proper handwashing techniques and cover their mouths and noses while coughing or sneezing. Avoid exposure to sick individuals and crowded places during flu seasons.

3. Managing Allergies

Allergies can significantly impact a child's quality of life. Identify and manage allergies by avoiding triggers and seeking medical advice if necessary. Keep the home environment clean and dust-free to reduce allergen exposure.

4. Addressing Digestive Issues

Digestive problems like constipation are common in children. Encourage a fiber-rich diet, sufficient hydration, and regular physical activity to promote healthy digestion. Consult a pediatrician if digestive issues persist.

5. Handling Common Injuries

Children are prone to accidents and injuries during play. Teach them basic safety rules and supervise their activities. In the event of an injury, provide immediate first aid and seek medical attention when needed.

Fostering Healthy Habits

1. Establishing Healthy Eating Habits

Introduce a variety of nutritious foods early in a child's life. Avoid processed and sugary foods, and focus on a balanced diet with adequate vitamins and minerals. Encourage family meals and set a positive example by eating healthily yourself.

2. Promoting Hydration

Staying hydrated is crucial for children's physical health and cognitive function. Provide access to water throughout the day and limit sugary beverages. Carry water bottles when going out to encourage regular hydration.

3. Prioritizing Sleep

Adequate sleep is vital for a child's growth and development. Set a consistent bedtime routine and ensure they get enough sleep based on their age requirements. Create a calm and comfortable sleep environment to promote restful sleep.

4. Teaching Personal Hygiene

Good personal hygiene habits are essential for preventing the spread of germs and maintaining overall health. Teach children to wash their hands regularly, brush their teeth, and keep their personal belongings clean.

5. Emotional Well-being and Stress Management

Promote emotional well-being by encouraging open communication and providing a supportive environment. Teach stress management techniques like deep breathing, mindfulness, and engaging in hobbies they enjoy.

Conclusion

Nurturing physical health in children is a multi-faceted responsibility that involves encouraging physical activity, dealing with common illnesses, and fostering healthy habits. By creating an environment that prioritizes active play, balanced nutrition, and emotional well-being, we set our children on a path to a healthy and fulfilling life. As caregivers, parents, and educators, our efforts in nurturing their physical health will have a lasting impact on their overall development and well-being. Let us strive to provide them with the best foundation possible for a happy and healthy childhood.

Chapter 15. School Years and Beyond
Preparing for school, academic support, and fostering lifelong learning

Introduction

The school years mark a crucial phase in a child's life, shaping their academic, social, and emotional development. As parents and caregivers, it is our responsibility to provide the necessary support to ensure children flourish during their educational journey and beyond. In this comprehensive guide, we will explore essential aspects of preparing children for school, providing academic support, and fostering a love for lifelong learning.

Preparing for School

1. Early Education and Preschool

Early education and preschool play a fundamental role in preparing children for the transition to formal schooling. It provides a structured environment where they can develop essential skills, including social interaction, emotional regulation, and basic cognitive abilities. Engaging in activities that promote creativity and curiosity enhances their overall readiness for school.

2. Establishing Routines

Consistency is key during the early school years. Creating and maintaining daily routines can instill a sense of security and predictability in children's lives. A well-structured routine helps them manage time effectively, fostering a sense of responsibility and independence. It also includes establishing regular sleep patterns, promoting optimal physical and mental health.

3. Encouraging Independence

Encourage your child to take on age-appropriate responsibilities, fostering a sense of independence. Allow them to make choices, solve problems, and complete tasks on their own. This independence builds their confidence and self-esteem, essential attributes for success in school and beyond.

4. Emotional Readiness

Emotional readiness is just as important as academic readiness when preparing for school. Help your child develop emotional intelligence by validating their feelings, teaching coping strategies, and fostering empathy towards others. A child who can navigate their emotions is better equipped to handle the challenges of school life.

5. Social Skills Development

Social skills are vital for establishing meaningful relationships and creating a positive school experience. Organize playdates (planned social gatherings where children get together to play and interact with their peers in a supervised and structured setting), involve your child in group activities, and promote healthy communication to develop their social competence. Building strong interpersonal skills helps children adapt to different social settings and form lasting friendships.

Academic Support

1. Identifying Individual Learning Styles

Each child has a unique learning style. Some may excel through visual aids, while others learn best through auditory or kinesthetic (understanding and processing information through physical activities and hands-on experiences) methods. Observe your child's preferences and adapt their learning environment to cater to their specific style. This understanding can significantly enhance their comprehension and retention of information.

2. Communication with Teachers

Open communication with teachers is vital for monitoring a child's academic progress. Attend parent-teacher conferences regularly to gain insights into your child's strengths and areas that need improvement. Collaborate with educators to develop personalized learning strategies and address any challenges promptly.

3. Homework and Study Habits

Encourage consistent study habits from an early age. Create a designated study area free from distractions, establish a homework routine, and be available to assist with assignments. Teach your child time-management skills and the importance of staying organized to enhance their academic performance.

4. Additional Academic Support

Some children may require additional academic support beyond the regular classroom environment. Identify any learning difficulties early on and seek professional assistance, such as tutoring or special education programs. Early intervention can make a significant difference in a child's academic journey.

5. Promoting a Growth Mindset

Foster a growth mindset by encouraging your child to embrace challenges, persist in the face of setbacks, and view failures as opportunities to learn. A growth mindset cultivates a love for learning and instills resilience, enabling children to achieve their full potential.

Fostering Lifelong Learning

1. Cultivating Curiosity

Nurture your child's innate curiosity by exposing them to diverse experiences and subjects. Encourage them to ask questions, explore their interests, and pursue new knowledge. A curious mind remains open to learning opportunities throughout life.

2. Reading and Literacy

Reading is the gateway to knowledge and imagination. Cultivate a love for reading by engaging in storytelling, visiting libraries, and creating a home environment that celebrates books. Encourage discussions about what they read to enhance comprehension and critical thinking skills.

3. Experiential Learning

Hands-on experiences enrich a child's learning journey. Engage in field trips, experiments, and practical activities that complement classroom learning. Experiential learning fosters a deeper understanding of concepts and encourages creativity.

4. Emphasizing the Value of Education

Communicate the value of education and its impact on their future. Help your child set academic goals and celebrate their achievements. Understanding the significance of education motivates children to take their learning seriously.

5. Role Modeling Lifelong Learning

Be a role model for lifelong learning by displaying a curious and proactive approach to gaining knowledge. Share your learning experiences with your child, demonstrating that education is a continuous journey that extends beyond formal schooling.

Conclusion

The school years are a critical period for laying the foundation of a child's academic and personal development. By preparing them for school, offering academic support, and fostering a love for lifelong learning, we equip our children with the tools they need to thrive academically and lead fulfilling lives as curious, resilient, and self-motivated learners. Remember that every child is unique, so adapt these strategies to suit their individual needs, strengths, and interests. With our unwavering support, they will confidently navigate the challenges and opportunities that lie ahead.

Introduction

Parenting is undoubtedly one of the most rewarding experiences, but it can also be incredibly challenging and demanding. As parents and caregivers, our focus is often centered on ensuring the well-being and development of our children. In the process of nurturing their growth, we may unknowingly neglect our own well-being. However, it is essential to recognize that taking care of ourselves is equally vital for being effective and compassionate caregivers. This article explores the concept of parental self-care and highlights its significance in promoting healthy child development and overall family harmony.

Understanding Parental Self-Care

Parental self-care refers to the practice of intentionally taking time to look after one's physical, emotional, and mental well-being amidst the responsibilities and demands of parenting. It involves engaging in activities that promote relaxation, personal growth, and stress reduction. Many parents may feel guilty or selfish for prioritizing their own needs, but it is crucial to understand that self-care is not a luxury but a necessity.

The Importance of Parental Self-Care

1. Enhanced Parent-Child Relationship

When parents take care of themselves, they are better equipped to build stronger connections with their children. Self-care fosters emotional regulation, patience, and empathy, allowing parents to respond more positively to their children's needs. A well-balanced parent is more likely to engage in active listening and open communication, creating a safe and supportive environment for the child's emotional development.

2. Role Modeling Healthy Behavior

Children learn by observing their parents' actions. By practicing self-care, parents demonstrate the value of taking care of oneself and prioritizing mental and physical well-being. This sets a positive example for children and instills in them the importance of self-care as they grow into adulthood.

3. Reduced Parental Stress

Parenting can be overwhelming, and chronic stress can lead to burnout and exhaustion. Engaging in self-care activities can significantly reduce stress levels, enabling parents to better manage the daily challenges of parenting. Reduced stress contributes to a healthier family dynamic and prevents potential negative impacts on the child's emotional well-being.

4. Increased Patience and Tolerance

Parental self-care cultivates emotional resilience, making parents more patient and understanding in challenging situations. When parents take time to recharge and decompress, they can respond calmly to difficult behaviors and conflicts, fostering a nurturing and supportive atmosphere within the family.

Strategies for Effective Parental Self-Care

1. Prioritizing Personal Time

Allocate dedicated time each day or week for self-care activities, such as reading, exercise, meditation, or pursuing hobbies. Setting aside this time and treating it as non-negotiable will ensure that parents prioritize their well-being.

2. Establishing Supportive Networks

Seek support from family, friends, or parenting groups. Building a network of like-minded individuals provides opportunities for sharing experiences, seeking advice, and receiving emotional support, all of which are vital for parental well-being.

3. Regular Exercise

Physical activity is not only beneficial for the body but also has a positive impact on mental health. Incorporating regular exercise into daily routines can boost mood, reduce stress, and improve overall well-being.

4. Mindfulness and Meditation

Practicing mindfulness and meditation can help parents stay present in the moment, reduce anxiety, and improve emotional regulation. Taking a few minutes each day to meditate or practice deep breathing exercises can have significant benefits.

5. Engaging in Creative Outlets

Encourage parents to engage in creative activities they enjoy, such as painting, writing, or playing musical instruments. These outlets can provide a sense of fulfillment and act as a form of therapeutic expression.

6. Adequate Sleep

Adequate sleep is crucial for physical and mental health. Parents should strive to establish healthy sleep routines and ensure they are getting enough rest each night.

Overcoming Barriers to Parental Self-Care

1. Guilt and Self-Judgment

Many parents may experience guilt when taking time for themselves, feeling they should always be focused on their children's needs. It is essential to understand that self-care is not selfish; it is an essential aspect of being an effective caregiver.

2. Time Constraints

Parenting often leaves little time for personal pursuits. However, parents can integrate self-care into their daily routines by making small but meaningful changes, such as waking up a bit earlier or utilizing break times during the day.

3. Financial Constraints

Self-care does not necessarily require expensive activities. Many low-cost or free options, such as nature walks, reading, or journaling, can be just as effective in promoting well-being.

4. Lack of Support

Parents who lack a support system may find it challenging to find time for self-care. In such cases, reaching out to community resources, online support groups, or seeking professional counseling can be beneficial.

Conclusion

Parental self-care is not a luxury but a fundamental aspect of effective caregiving and fostering healthy child development. By recognizing the importance of their well-being, parents can create a nurturing environment for both themselves and their children. Prioritizing self-care enables parents to better cope with challenges, model healthy behaviors, and establish stronger connections with their children. By taking the time to care for themselves, parents are better equipped to care for their children, resulting in a happier and more harmonious family life.

"The Complete Guide to Child Development and Care" is a comprehensive and invaluable resource for parents and caregivers, offering expert insights into every stage of a child's growth. From the early days of parenthood, Chapter 1 delves into the vital role parents and caregivers play in shaping a child's life. Ensuring a safe and nurturing environment is explored in Chapter 2, providing essential tips on childproofing and creating a child-friendly home. Chapters 3 and 4 cover the intricacies of caring for a newborn and nurturing infants, emphasizing bonding, communication, and emotional needs. As children progress, Chapter 5 highlights the significance of healthy nutrition, while Chapter 6 focuses on understanding toddler development and employing positive discipline techniques. Recognizing the importance of play in Chapter 7, the book presents age-appropriate activities and the impact of play on a child's development.

Preparing children for preschool, fostering language skills, and promoting emotional intelligence are elaborated in Chapters 8 and 9. Chapter 10 offers effective discipline strategies with empathy, and Chapter 11 explores ways to inspire creativity and artistic expression in children. Chapters 13 and 14 cover healthy sleep habits and nurturing physical health, providing guidance on maintaining an active lifestyle and addressing common illnesses. As children enter school age, Chapter 15 assists in preparing them for academic success and fostering lifelong learning. Finally, Chapter 16 emphasizes the significance of parental self-care and its impact on the overall well-being of both parents and caregivers. This book serves as an indispensable companion, empowering readers with the knowledge and tools to navigate the rewarding journey of child development and care with confidence and love.

ABOUT THE AUTHOR

Mr. C. P. Kumar is a retired Scientist 'G' from National Institute of Hydrology, Roorkee, Uttarakhand, India. He is also a Reiki Healer and Chakra Balancing practitioner (with pendulum dowsing) and offers Emotional Freedom Technique (EFT) to help individuals with emotional issues. Mr. Kumar has authored many books on technical, spiritual, and social topics.

For further details, you may visit his webpage
https://www.angelfire.com/nh/cpkumar/virgo.html